Twenty-Four Covers
of a House on Fire

poems by

C. Henry Smith

Finishing Line Press
Georgetown, Kentucky

Twenty-Four Covers of a House on Fire

ACKNOWLEDGMENTS

Excerpts from this poem have been included in *The Paddock Review* and
Driftwood Press' 2025 Anthology.

Publisher: Leah Huete de Maines
Editor: Christen Kincaid
Cover Art: C. Henry Smith
Author Photo: C. Henry Smith
Cover Design: Elizabeth Maines McCleavy

Order online: www.finishinglinepress.com
also available on amazon.com

Author inquiries and mail orders:
Finishing Line Press
PO Box 1626
Georgetown, Kentucky 40324
USA

For Tom

The barroom's closed after midnight, Hank. Pasture-bound, the
cattle low. Let's weather this lonesome like quail-doves,
consider

the Christmas tree shrouded in flames, the tin angels, what
uncorralled stars marked the evening, the evening of the
blaze,

or an age before streetlamps, home and its endless landscape,
how the evening meant an end to the day, the effort of
days and sweating,

it meant the onset of homebound trains when the snow could
begin to fall. There are geese that don't notice the
floodwater, Hank. Slugs that miss the tornado.

And how a house may bear its disasters. A body may. What other
structures, Hank, what animals are my body?

What is my body in this new city so unwintered, so distant from
the twisters, housefires, the bright calamities of home,

the Haunted Lady of Lefors, good bruises the color of horsefall?
Hank, this city is honking. Nobody is listening home. I
cannot stop thinking about the sundown cattle. Teach
me:

one wonder, one prosper in your staying. Home. What's earned
simple at the origin. Teach me: your dream life, the saints
that make a showing, the color

your voice takes in a chapel wind, what season after season keeps
you spur-dug and tripping

prairie dog chambers, the thrown horseshoes of an earnest linger.
Hank, I'm bleeding attention, drive, slim paychecks, and
though the water is good,

there's never enough to go Christening. I am learning the shape
my body takes in an artificial light. I am. Dancing.

I dance like records two-step about a jukebox, like the flaming
pages of desire float up, up into the skyline.

4

Hank, what's east of desire? Where the country ends in
    December, milk trucks roll contentedly into the sea?

There is apostic intent in my wandering, my nightly disease,
    Hank. I run, and I remember our city's last dinerette,
    marking wounded jake brakes, heat mirage,

the Marlboro Red 100s, and inside, the oil hands, rig bosses, the
    off-season farmer who wondered why no one heated
    syrup

on the stove like his mother had while he finished his homework
    at the breakfast table, homework he swore was finished
    the night before,

problem sets and Italian verbs, arguing with his sister until they
    had to split the odd piece of bacon.

A fistful of dollars, Hank. The ritual, how everyone in the
    smoking section takes their eggs, white

runny or Vantablack. Turn kind away, that they might bourbon
    their coffee at last, that the sticky bills of shift life might
    translate

into something graspable as the walk-in's release lever. I miss
    strangers, Hank, regulars, the identity of person as relates
    to place. I miss smoke breaks,

even a five between seatings to kiss my fingers, watch the sun rise,
    breathe something toxic, tangible out into the bug light.

+

The landscape of endurance is fluorescent. I'm told there are
        sunsets in this city, Hank, not the perfect bloodbath,
        murdered grapefruits of home,

but a kind of balm light between the skyscrapers. I long for a
        well-lit redemption. Twelve minutes on either side of the
        day to remember my place in all things.

It's something to do with the candles, Hank. A Camel Gold
        ember and the fairy lights lassoing the doorframe. The
        atmosphere

of Slim's monthly party, it has become the party I throw myself,
        night after night, in my psalterium, my middling space
        between

the Hereford's mouth and tail. The cherry-tailed trainline in the
        window, Hank. That Uptown apartment, its enduring
        cell phone

blink, Santos, the aura over the microphone, two-handed time
        on the stove. I dream in lost light,

in an amassing of warmer colors, and I think of my siblings in an
        ice storm around the artificial hearth,

motel cartoons after flooding, of the car crash daylight an hour
        past the tornado, or the strands of green and red that
        flickered, enduring after our holiday fire.

4

Hank, it helps that you're here. To feel one body less lonely, to
    practice the motions we'll make, one day, as ghosts:

tattooed clavicles knocking, rickety shrug of chains. Which way,
    Hank? Death by indecision, death by everlasting faint,
    death by drifting

too far out in still waters. I once swam with my brother out in still
    waters—the sea, Hank, the sea. The quality of light. Our
    uncle taught us to dive and blow warm air out a snorkel

so we could shift from the sun to the coral effortlessly, in the right
    tide, in the right summer, in a clarity of intention so far
    from the lakefronts,

the gulf oil, the dirty bathwaters of home. Our tanned skin. Salted
    eyes. It is an admission, Hank, of maturity, to last abiding
    between two shores. Stasis

and the in-between, they're all that can keep me from sleeping. I
    can't last, abide, weather, stay. The exit—it's all I can
    cotton. I can't manage to shake

my autumn coat off at parties or leave behind my vehicle when
    we're carpooling to the Campbell's Hayhook Ranch. I am
    roaming backward through life

one cowgate at a time, spitting liquor, falling up porch steps,
    kissing lips away. Perhaps I started as ghost.

Perhaps we all started as ghost, and that explains why we're so
    good at absence. Slipping through each other, branding it
    embrace.

4

I can only survive with an addressee, Hank. With the green and
    gold teeth of meaning pulled out and nestled

in the garden of another. I'm dusting off the days, looking away
    from the clapboard horizon.

Once there was time. Space. Hank. Something caprock-sized and
    bucking underneath, the blizzards late as Easter,

wildflower season, dances at the rodeo grounds, high school
    lights on Fridays that bled out for miles.

Or rinderpest, bluetongue, hoof and mouth, and how the
    highway department would dispose of carcasses tossed
    over the fence line.

There was tragedy, majesty every sundown. Oh, we're cheated
    out of so much orange here, Hank. Out of Sunday
    company and sky.

It should be enough to be From. To be Headed. Just to Be. Any
    measure of it, Hank,

should quilt-cover the full cot and come with a pillow, should at
    least be rent-stabilized. It is too much here among the
    living.

Everyone expects so much out of life. And everyone back home,
    not enough. Oh, watch,

I'll wax, Hank. Wax under the bar light until I can ride the cows
    back home. Make it to magic hour underneath the
    clothesline.

4

Or the rodeo, carnival, cookout, fair. Can't find them, Hank, in
     this incognita terra. Here, I can't find myself, any
     memory of garland, ritual burning. No,

I won't make it on the modern midway. The attractions, less
     stable lately. The games get tougher with age—all leave
     you prizeless, sore,

and curious why you laid your tip-earned dollars down. I never
     felt my physique could integrate

with the constructs around it, the coffee hour, cash box, roller
     coaster, landscape. Humans most of all. But still, I keep
     reaching toward another

body or the milk bottles deceptively arranged. Hank, the
     language of the body is truest, the words found
     everywhere but the throat. I can't help

being shaped like an oil derrick decaying. A crucifix, a scythe. I
     worship like a water moccasin slides easy into the river. I
     collapse

my body when the world presents more than I first imagined. My
     canyon eyes. My body, Hank, demands that I listen,

let it dream beyond itself. How it is my best instrument. How it
     moves me unexpected through this world.

+

My teardrop brim body, Hank, paint its shutters. Rub its gills.
 And for dinner, mix metaphors even further, spill on
 generous tequila, queso. The riverbed's salted rim ever
 drying.

I am managing, stretching, a lean toward something like
 satisfaction, what went unbuttered in, forgive me,

the biscuits of home. It is only honeysuckle and the honey daisy.
 Milkweed, calliopsis, desert wave.

Not enough to pepper the days. Or too much. Or a watering the
 bud at the back of the neck, root

lips like you'd use to kiss caliche, camel-colored fracking, the
 promise of well water or oil.

Hank, this longing for thunderbolt terrain, its legacy, the bad
 hours, all contrary as the flavor of catfish knowing what
 fills its insides.

I've filled mine gummy. To weather, to become slowly flooded,
 Hank. Sud soothed and bourboned, hidden,

mash ruddy. I soften, dampen nostalgia, unbottle the missing
 parts. I feel it, Hank. My throat has lost its landscape.
✛

So where do you physic holy, Hank? Your body, awake and
    counting in the sorghum, its six-string draw in swing
    time, in fall,

in the five corners of your Gray County downtown stretching for
    the sleepwalk back home,

in the train tracks and the drug store where Woody learned to
    pluck and mew. The streetlamp décor: candy canes,
    rodeo broncs,

the green and gold Harvester—all sponsored by the city banker's
    community bureau. An unspoken assertion that home

would make a great big SomeThing out of NoThing, Hank, would
    cook powder kegs in back of the old ceramics shop.

The fire escape behind Ice Cream & More what leads you where
    any staircased sentence leads: the bottom or top of desire,

a good scrape in the gutter, rooftop psalms in Old English. And
    down Cuyler Ave, the red wagon clacking over cement
    teeth,

southern Christine Street, a junior runaway's kit: socks and
    goldfish tied up in a bindle, a box of colored pencils,

and a warm glass of milk. Dad followed at a safe distance in his
    evergreen truck, shot

dead the doves from the trees. The real runaway at seventeen.
        State-wide reprise at twenty-one.

+

You ask me how escape has been, Hank, and I long to
    understand your remain. Our run count coruscating
    between the home team, the away.

Confide in me then: do your whiskey teeth and trophy figurines
    still pitch about the middle of your head? Confide,

and I'll talk Old Overholt in the chapel ignition, free-throws up
    and down the interstate, Historical Marker, Passing
    Ahead,

The Vast and Unimaginable Present, Cemetery Left, everything
    haunted in hideaway, in apostasy, rotting in place,

everything plowline and prairie, the text on the tombstone that
    fades. After, after. Wait, Hank. Wait.

We are from hunger, Hank. Hamms, a *handkerchief sandwich*,
    heart failure, and all that. We all are. From.

From rust-colored awnings, the pirate smiles in downtown
    bankers, and the horse thieves, their ancestors,

the plains thieves, our ancestors, and further back the line of
    tipping candles, one flame wicking into the next,

unlit back, back in time, wax reformed until infants are the
    thieves of God. Peace and rain, Hank. Cold hallelujah off
    of limestone.

✦

Help me attend to the living, Hank. I count myself among these.
Every day marks a new year and we're everlasting,
everlasting. In this year,

the following, the year of jackrabbits or snapdragons, the year of
harvesters or wind turbines. Tall saltgrass, honeysuckle
vines. Of landscape, Hank,

the possibilities of home after a housefire. An architecture of one's
own. Help me to get off the widow's walk, Hank.

I can't tell what I'm missing or mourning the way I stumble over
death like ghost cats on the back stairwell,

taking out the trash, leaving votives beneath the lindens. Paschal
candles. Altar candles. Brass acolyte torch and wick. The
problem is not so distant.

Is me, Hank. My home church and hometown were no crowd for
adverbs. Bring them up active. Merge. Kneel. Stay. So
glibly I've Hallelujah strayed.

And the housefire turned twenty-one this evening. The tornado,
twenty-nine, next June. I listen to the windchimes when I
visit the winter.

I talk to Southwestern rail cars just like they're Grand Central, ask
the station master when he'll chug off into the upset.
Nobody changed until this summer,

and now I think of Tom anytime I smell a Winston or someone
spends seventy years remodeling a house.

4

Hank, the nights might find me at parties despite my riding the
        other way. There is the good light, the people, but the
        people—oh, the people—

in downstairs apartments, upstairs, in the ballroom around the
        corner, in the hayloft, the grand Mercury Club rising,

the automat, the laundromat, the new condos by the train. My
        scope is so limited, Hank.

My body unable to make more than a mite's assumption about
        the size of this environment, this long crawl

of entrances, escapes. This tomorrow. Tomorrow. Then, now,
        Hank. I spend hours inside of a doorframe, just waiting
        for the host to blink or turn the other way,

for an excuse to go or an excuse to be seen, to be attended but
        never perceived, for the offer of a fried or a stuffed
        something, a toast, a prayer, a reason to hold fast, to
        sober, believe.

Why must we gather, Hank? Why is it not enough to be, to be
        one face not forced to contort like the circle of others,

to be dry without the slippery cocktails of gathering, to do alone
        the work, the mischief and the work, to never pause to
        blush at the living?

Bootcut, Hank. Bourbonous and waiting to pitch horseshoes, I
        picture you back home, circumnavigating society in a
        similar way,

like a coyote drawn to campfire reluctant out of the scrubland.
        What temperature must we reach, what palm offer,

how predator, how prey, how long does the party have to be
        sleeping for us to retire back into the darkness?

+

The way a house party's a house fire, Hank. In which part of the
    flame does my body look its best? Or who will ask my
    body in, give it keys to stay?

After the holiday housefire, a chiropractor from church took his
    home off the market, gave us keys for the year.

After the flood, it was the Coronado Motel. After the tornado, we
    walked the streets, saw where grass was stuck into trees.

After the separation, our parents divided the state. After Dad's
    ordination, divinity felt split the same.

I am inside a long series of locks, of clips and bolts stopping the
    light from crossing the keyhole. I am portraits of a
    medieval page, the hidden symbols,

the apostolic acts that didn't make it into print, the energy of
    being begun, the quixotic wind turbines, the bath of the
    sun,

the strange ordinaries, the curse of living sober, weltschmerz and
    ennui, Hank. I am a body restless, changed.

Hank, what do I make of missing keys, their shoeboxes, and the
    locks that have been changed? When I walk back from
    the train, I dig

the shoulder, cuts, and biting of my apartment key deep enough
    into my hand I could fabricate a replacement if jumped,
    if the grate mouth

over a subway swallowed this rented weight. I think endlessly
    about the word security, whether cure can fit inside.

4

My mother gifted keys, Hank, to the cupboard my father
fashioned, to the Midland house on Texas Ave,

skeletons from swap meets, junk shops, rummage sales, and the
vomited garage muddle on front lawns

viewable from early Friday through Sunday eve. There are not
garages large enough for what I want to release

nickel-tagged or OBO'd out into the wild, memories and gut-deep
things, eyes on my mother locking the apartment,

on my father locking himself religious away, my endless reach
into sundown, into the demon feet of my ancestors,
naming, naming,

the perishment of bison, the padlock of displacement. I reach,
Hank. I reach for my belt-clipped keyring like my cousin
reaches for her pistol.

I reach for bad pumpkins, cataract melons, middling carrots, flat
beans, everything that survived our mad dog's gnashing

inside the chain link garden locked out back. I reach eager for
stable things like stables, paddocks, those half-cut doors
for conversations with horses

what kept kids secure in the church basement nursery but let
parents peek in before the liturgy.

✝

It sounds just like a story, Hank, where it is raining somewhere
on the East Coast, not where I am, but in the fixed
picture

window behind my therapist. And he listens, on camera, as I talk
about the church basement nursery what kept us until
communion,

the unfinished mural of storm clouds, Noah, and every creature
beholden unto the ark. In this story, I, too, am beholden.

In every story, beholden. In this session, I want to discuss the
toys gifted from the children of dead parishioners:

church nursery toys kept in paint buckets, in laundry baskets,
tooth-marked milk crates. Broken playthings my
brother, sister, and I could pull after the weekly coloring
sheet—

Belshazzar's candle settings, the neon angel chasing Mary. And
when the rain picks up on my therapist's Zoom screen,

and the window in the window gets darker, I describe the toy I
still taste, Hank, I still feel dreaming, waking, against my
ear always:

the plastic pair of phone receivers, the handsets, hay golden and
joined by a springless line. Here, I see through the
camera that my therapist is sleeping.

4

The story rains on, Hank. Ritual. It is ritual when I place one
handset in the nursery corner beneath sponge-painted
clouds,

a rainbow's origin swirl that I take to mean *God*, when I sit with
the other end talking the half-hour before Mom plucks
us,

one phone pressing a crescent into my temple, the other phone
calling out to heaven above, calling about catechism class
that morning, my coat hook

at the real school, my parents upstairs, late-night, Saturday AM
Captain Planet, trains, and Virgin Mary, about the gift
my grandparents make

of an olive tree when I turned five. And I ask for things. An older
sibling, for quiet, what the adults want: peace and rain,

a Dole presidency, the right combination of numbers to align on
a Wednesday night. One good yaw in the price of oil.

And I close my eyes, listen for anything more than rain, rattle
the handset, watch the clouds darken, see the bodies in
the floodwater, squeeze.

+

No, nothing resembles a stable place, Hank. Nothing holds a
    body in the ways it wants to be. Held. Remembered. I
    spend days among the data farmers,

market ranchers, no one who knows my mother's name. I tell
    them about fire, flood, tornado—they ask if I've updated
    the webpage.

Unfounded, unfound, I call to you then, Hank. I call later, call
    now to the version of me that stayed, never missed the
    pasture,

never saw in the skyline a canyon while driving down the Joe
    DiMaggio Highway, so underwhelmed by the landscape,

the ferry-boats, flood-tide, clouds, containers that belong on the
    flatbed of a flatcar. I ride the rails out here, Hank.

F, Q, G, A. At astronomical twilight the sun is wrecked on the
    surface of the water. It cannot stay, cannot find a surface
    of stable reflection.

I pause for a moment of reflection. I hold both sides of the
    Hudson, try to remember how to pray. I need something
    to be coming, Hank, or I need

soil to fill my shoes, reason to remain, the way my grandmother
    always asked me to hang on after supper, help my
    grandfather in the attic, put out the Christmas
    decorations.

4

I wade beyond satisfaction, Hank. Unlike a child, need more than
warm milk and a name.

I need more than a cigarette or an absinthe shake, a keyhole tutor,
one banderole at the end of a post.

It's Ogallala water, Mom's bedtime narratives, rockfoil blooms,
Sister's jokes, and afternoon thunderstorms most of all.

Tell me what's desirable in the present, Hank. In the post-
calamity hiccup where longing can unravel, listening can
begin.

Something muddy concerning car rental agreements, vanity
metrics, bar tabs, the whole slam. Lots to juggle to be
alive.

And I'm trying to see. To really see. To tend to the sparks on my
own work coat, not the ones three months down pasture,

but I'm ablaze with something water can't cure: a malt barrel
tingle, the north transept organ's D flat, dry branch
passages of badland desire.

Brush in the right hand, stick in the left, shots in the glove box,
engine-greased flaps.

What I don't know about homeplace and belonging, sobriety and
cars, Hank, could fill at least a freight train.

+

I faltered after the fire, Hank. Suspected after flood, tornado,
    divorce, quake, religion, flame that home couldn't haven
    our being,

our heart would one day disappear regular as the evening train—
    bend riverly, deteriorate, flash sinister before swallowed
    into the starlight.

Last night, the party faltered at the local engine blast. Blowsy
    cocktail in the right hand, tracks in the left,

the train drum sounding so close to the balcony, we tied our
    laces together, swore not to jump.

Molly paused the horror movie, nobody could speak. Each of us
    suddenly in our own childhood bedroom, listening to a
    parent's stories or the back gate unlatch.

Listening for the 6:15 and the 11, their splash in the container of
    night. The big lonely in escape. We all know

what it's like to let memory barrel by, resist the urge to let it kill
    you. I'm writing today from a distance:

the fringes of the fringes of the fringe. Hank, what's a good
    boxcar word for this instant

that is no more present now than the future or the past, what
    anticipates the version of us passed, remembers the
    version that will come?

Like a hooting, Hank, a squat owl's, *Who?* The train sound, the
    train's sound. The train is sound. The trains sound. The
    trains' sound. The train, sound.

Time uncoils like a well-wound saddle line. We can only chase
    the calf one delivery at a time.

4

Hank, let's weigh desire on a livestock scale. Hoof to tail, the
impulse toward escape. The impulse toward a victory
purse containing

me and civil twilight and the car seats and bad habits, their
inflections, self-afflictions, with how many pounds of
force I can push a body away.

Living with a legacy, Hank. A pinch and purloin legacy. From
Adam down, slaughter and nomenclature. The sum
weight,

I don't like the enumeration, the hands and face reflected in the
TI-83 beneath me. I keep thinking of the plains greatness

I'll rediscover near the end. Tall native grasses. A season full of
cattle, Hank. I've grown romantic about

the cattle. I'll untie the four legs of return, but only after staying
long enough away I can never meet a non-stranger

except in the back of the Walmart, searching for discounted bait,
barbless fishhooks per the game warden's regulation,

or some sense of place. I would get lost in the supermarket as a
child. It's so dreamlike now, never wanting to be found.

+

Hank, I'm not the rodeo clown I seek to be. No arena or chute
    line bull rush, no greasepaint, no narrative of purpose to
    contain me. Lo, let somebody contain me. Some

body. Contain me without a promise of labor or payment. Barter
    holding for holding. Today, a new bee season starts
    without

work boots on BOGO sale. And all we are out here is market,
    Hank. Inside, outside, just data-pointed footprints with a
    ripe junk folder.

When I worked for Tom, we'd drive 45 minutes to his property
    every morning just to talk with a dying horse, spray
    paint

new plans for his collapsing ranch house. From canyon then to
    Tom's long rooms back home, full of his mother's
    Western oil paintings

that he couldn't let go. He had it bad, Hank. A lifetime of try. We
    all go a long way to finance our own tombstone, to
    sustain our native cradles.

I consider my relationship with labor, systems. I consider myself
    in systems, a nag, a clown, or a worker bee inside larger
    systems. Let me participate or at least

commit helpful devilment at the rodeo. In our fractured Texas
    downtown, somebody wrote an ode to the nuthatch
    beneath the mural of Lady Liberty.

Now I see her daily, dividing the Hudson, how the water decides
    to jacket her, east or west, and I wonder what it feels like
    to be pressed against, cooled in that way.

4

Hank, I held on through half of a wedding. When my therapist
        asks about the state of my battery, I think about our first
        F-150,

how we are asked to utter holy, even when key turns to nothing. I
        hang on better back home, the spitfire, if Shakespearean,

combination of more characters, more problems. The O'Leary
        cow couldn't have started the fire, and I still picture her
        in Chicago praying,

holding back the crowd against her cattle, herding the blame
        toward herself. Hank, is home active or passive love? The
        people, the big, easy targets,

the droughts full of sleep. In the wedding I fall asleep, I descend,
        recept within a ballroom at tables made of numbers,

in situations where I'm called on to exist among the gift-giving,
        the wool-tied, the smart-watched, the loving, those who
        believe

in love, in a kind of love that can be jumped into action by ritual,
        kicked into spark by a well-tended cow, love

that means more than history, precedent, statistic. Biology,
        pessimism, idolatry, chance. I am lonely in my poor
        positions. I am lonely in a space

where so long as we keep on dancing, everything is going to be
        ok. The F-150 we bought from a substitute teacher, Dad
        sold it before the divorce.

Matched jackets, matched flowers, the old pantheon from college.
        Thou talk'st of nothing. Thou talk'st of nothing.

+

It's something to do with homeplace, Hank, blood harmonies,
and the lot. I remember when I learned about absence

in arithmetic, the late addition to Western numeracy, the zero,
what it means to begin wanting.

It's something to do with desire, but remembering forward,
longing back. I can't remember what direction the Ford
F-150 Lariat was pointed,

only that I never traveled with chains, loved the sensation of
wheels polishing ice, troutlike at every stop. Maybe it's
more to do with wriggle,

resisting the slow down and whatever nature has plunked
beneath the tires. Hank, I am tired.

I have had so many jobs. My labor feels stranger to my self. I
have lived so many places. Help me to know my body,

my constants, my times tables, and where the jack, after the
changing, goes in the car's three-part belly.

Help me turn my desire back inwards for manageable things like
breath, metabolizing, the way platelets merengue as
shoals of fish

down their narrow, middle school hallways. My veins, the
swimming, Hank. A channel for the tiny and miraculous
life inside.

+

Hank. Hank, I don't need to know that you're listening, only that
     you'll stay. Together let's consider a prairie of warrens,

the jackrabbit warrens, our warrens, the scarred mullion and
     pollen remainder on the windowsill, the echo of
     nightlights welled inside.

Let's remember how the red rocks shaped and showed us time in
     their decay, a long-compacted life, more violets in the
     epochs

than we witnessed in Tom's paintings. My body shows time in its
     greying, in new folds and arrangements of fenceposts and
     aches.

Every day I long for a kind of comfort, someone to close their
     hands around mine in nautical twilight, to remind me
     the proper ranch-to-market turns.

How many funeral directors have been mayor in our hometown,
     Hank? Cattlemen? Priests? It is peaceful in the river. My
     body feels

peaceful in the river. The steady press of something to hold it. The
     light that comes from beneath, off German browns and
     rainbow trout, the rocks we slipped on as children.

It extraordinarily is, Hank. Living. Is. In this and everything else.
     Straining the body beyond the limits of the tall grass, the
     pinnated grouse, the play of cowlight against the horizon.

✝

We could all do with a final dousing, Hank. That flicker of
      wonder: water or gasoline? Hank, you have survived a
      household on fire,

the fond scalds, the knife, the late train in another's waiting
      room, neon desire, the smoke heaps that we remain
      alone in, together.

Let us give the world, Hank. Let us. Let the world be given. I
      remember the pall, paten, chalice, the needlework cross
      on the veil,

the ritual that sustained us. Hank. I want to feel sustained,
      inelegant, common, champagne tawdry in the cheap
      seats,

longed for, a longing, like I might belong, be long in a place
      worth being, to be parched and then soothed by the cool

and green stitch of another. The burden of others, of all of it.
      Hank, let that rucksack be enough. Let your boot color,

let the depth of hands into the dirt road past the farmhouse, let
      your tip jar, let the pushcart back home,

let the blue glass bottles, the horseshoe on every door, the record
      full of rodeo sounds that sent us off to sleep as kids.

At the end of the world, Hank, the old emcee will say, *And here is*
      my favorite sound of all, boys and girls, the song of the
      sleeping cattle,

and the needle will lift, and the stars won't have a thing to say,
      and we, we will already be dreaming.

C. Henry Smith is the author of the poetry chapbooks *Warren* (Ghost City Press) and *Twenty-Four Covers of a House on Fire* (Finishing Line Press), and his Pushcart and Best of the Net nominated work has appeared in *Colorado Review, DMQ Review, Psaltery & Lyre, LIT,* and others. He received his BA at St. Edward's University and his MFA at Oregon State University, and he is grateful for past residencies through Spring Creek Project and Chicago Art Department.

Smith began writing poetry at a young age and finds themes from juvenilia continue to crop up in his work—the physical and emotional landscape of home, masculinity, privilege, belonging, identity. As the child of a priest, his writing is also attentive to the lives of saints, mythology, and the place ritual holds in our daily lives, both the mundane and the miraculous. A religious upbringing also orients his writing towards death and imagined ways of being outside of the physical state.

As an educator, Chris has taught courses in theatre with Texas Arts Project and in writing at Oregon State University where he was managing editor of *45th Parallel Literary Magazine.* He has spoken at conferences on sustainable community development and the state of arts education. He also enjoys producing theatre, touching grass, volunteering, and asking strangers for their ghost stories.

www.ingramcontent.com/pod-product-compliance
Lightning Source LLC
Chambersburg PA
CBHW022103080426
42734CB00009B/1473